Language Literacy Lessons

Reading

Elementary

by Imogene Forte

Incentive Publications, Inc.
Nashville, Tennessee

Illustrated by Gayle S. Harvey
Cover Art by Rebecca Rüegger
Edited by Jean K. Signor

ISBN 0-86530-569-2

PRINTED IN THE UNITED STATES OF AMERICA
www.incentivepublications.com

Table of Contents

Comprehension and Independent Reading Skills 43

Appendix 75

HOW TO USE THIS BOOK

Achieving language literacy is a major benchmark in the education of every student in today's classrooms. Without reading, writing, speaking, and listening literacy the process of learning becomes increasingly difficult and the limits placed on academic achievement become more entrenched and solidified each year.

In the information saturated and technology dependent world of today, it is especially important for children to gain and be able to make meaningful use of the skills associated with language literacy at an early age. Success in content-based studies such as Math, Social Studies, and Science, and even in enrichment fields including Art, Music, and Literature are highly dependent on language literacy proficiency. With strong language skills, a student's academic future has fewer bounds and individual goals, expectancies and dreams stand a better chance of being realized. It was with respect for the importance of achieving a high level of language literacy for every student that the Language Literacy Lessons Series was developed.

The purpose of *Language Literacy Lessons: Reading, Elementary* is to help students achieve the desired literacy milestone through reinforcement of key language skills. The activities in this book have all been designed to provide student practice of essential reading skills. A skills checklist on page 10 details the skills covered. This skills checklist has been carefully gleaned from attention to research related to language while specific skills associated with each lesson are correlated to the age appropriate language literacy checklist.

Through the use of the lessons in this book, students will be advancing individual language literacy skills while working toward national standards! For help in lesson planning, an easy-to-use matrix on pages 8 and 9 presents National Language Arts Standards correlations for each lesson in the book.

Not only are the activities correlated to essential literacy skills and National Language Arts Standards, they are imaginative and their open-ended nature will prove to be engaging and of high-interest to students. Student creativity is tapped through intriguing situations to write about, interesting characters to read about, and captivating illustrations to inspire thoughtful student responses.

As language literacy skills improve, increased levels of overall school success will be readily apparent. Language literacy enables students to set achievable goals to go wherever their interests take them and to embark joyfully on a lifelong journey of learning!

STANDARDS MATRIX

STANDARD	ACTIVITY PAGE
Standard 1: Students read a wide range of print and nonprint text to build an understanding of texts, of themselves, and of the cultures of the United States and the world, to acquire new information, to respond to the needs and demands of society and the workplace, and for personal fulfillment. Among these texts are fiction and nonfiction, classic and contemporary works.	12, 30, 31, 38, 39, 40 53, 73
Standard 2: Students read a wide range of literature from many periods in many genres to build an understanding of the many dimensions (e.g., philosophical, ethical, aesthetic) of human experience.	26, 41, 51, 52
Standard 3: Students apply a wide range of strategies to comprehend, interpret, evaluate, and appreciate texts. They draw on their prior experience, their interactions with other readers and writers, their knowledge of word meaning and of other texts, their identification strategies, and their understanding of textual features (e.g., sound-letter correspondence, sentence structure, context, graphics).	13, 15, 44, 60, 62, 64
Standard 4: Students adjust their use of spoken, written, and visual language (e.g., conventions, style, vocabulary) to communicate effectively with a variety of audiences for a variety of purposes.	20, 21, 22, 42
Standard 5: Students employ a wide range of strategies as they write and use different writing process elements appropriately to communicate with different audiences for a variety of purposes.	23, 45, 57
Standard 6: Students apply knowledge of language structure, language conventions (e.g., spelling and punctuation), media techniques, figurative language, and genre to create, critique, and discuss print and non-print texts.	14, 16, 17, 18, 19, 24, 25, 27

(8)

Standards for the English Language Arts, by the International Reading Association and the National Council of Teachers of English, Copyright 1996 by the International Reading Association and the National Council of Teachers of English. Reprinted with permission.

Language Literacy Lessons / Writing Elementary
Copyright ©2002 by Incentive Publications, Inc.
Nashville, TN.

STANDARDS MATRIX

STANDARD	ACTIVITY PAGE
Standard 7: Students conduct research on issues and interests by generating ideas and questions, and by posing problems. They gather, evaluate, and synthesize data from a variety of sources (e.g., print and non-print texts, artifacts, people) to communicate their discoveries in ways that suit their purpose and audience.	32, 37, 54, 58, 59, 69, 71
Standard 8: Students use a variety of technological and informational resources (e.g., libraries, databases, computer networks, video) to gather and synthesize information and to create and communicate knowledge.	47, 48, 49, 61, 70
Standard 9: Students develop an understanding of and respect for diversity in language use, patterns, and dialects across cultures, ethnic groups, geographic regions, and social roles.	33, 68, 65, 72
Standard 10: Students whose first language is not English make use of their first language to develop competency in the English language arts and to develop understanding of content across the curriculum.	34, 35, 36, 55, 56, 65
Standard 11: Students participate as knowledgeable, reflective, creative, and critical members of a variety of literacy communities.	46, 50, 74, 76
Standard 12: Students use spoken, written, and visual language to accomplish their own purposes (e.g., for learning, enjoyment, persuasion, and the exchange of information).	28, 29, 63, 66, 67

Language Literacy Lessons / Writing Elementary
Copyright ©2002 by Incentive Publications, Inc.
Nashville, TN.

Standards for the English Language Arts, by the International Reading Association and the National Council of Teachers of English, Copyright 1996 by the International Reading Association and the National Council of Teachers of English. Reprinted with permission.

SKILLS CHECKLIST

	Demonstrates Visual Discrimination	12, 13
	Knows and Uses Short and Long Vowels	14
	Knows Beginning Sounds	15, 16
	Knows and Uses Consonant Blends	17, 18
	Knows and Can Use Phonics	19
	Recognizes Rhyming Words	20, 21, 22
	Knows and Can Use Rules for Syllabication	23
	Knows and Can Use Prefixes and Suffixes	24
	Can Use Contractions	26
	Can Use Compound Words	27
	Can Interpret Plurals	28, 29
	Can Use Sight Vocabulary	30
	Can Use Picture Clues	31
	Knows and Can Use Rebuses	32
	Can Use Context Clues	33
	Can Define Words by Classification	34, 35, 36
	Recognizes and Can Use Homonyms	37
	Can Interpret and Convey Meanings of a Variety of Familiar Words	38
	Can Recognize Word Relationships	39
	Can Use Descriptive Words	40, 41, 42
	Can Associate Words with Feelings	44
	Can Form Sensory Impressions	45, 46
	Can Use Picture and Idea Association	47
	Can Recall Information Read and Select Facts to Remember	48
	Is Able to Remember Details from Pictures	49
	Can Distinguish Between Fact and Opinion	50
	Can Find the Main Idea	51
	Can Identify Topic Sentences	52
	Can Read to Find Details	53, 54
	Can Arrange Ideas or Events in Sequence	55
	Can Draw Conclusions	56, 57, 58
	Can Distinguish Between Cause and Effect	59, 60
	Can Use the Dictionary	61
	Alphabetical Order	62
	Can Determine What Reference Source to Use, and Can Use Multiple Resources	63, 71
	Can Understand and Use Punctuation	64
	Can Follow Written Directions	65, 66, 67, 68, 69
	Can Take Notes from Reading	70
	Is Developing Reading Appreciation and Independence	72

Word Recognition and Usage Skills

Different Homes for Different Folks

Carpenter Jones built these two houses for the Johnson family and the Jackson family. Mrs. Jackson and Mrs. Johnson are lifelong friends, and wanted homes exactly alike.

Even though Mr. Jones prided himself on building "one-of-a-kind" homes, he agreed to build these two houses just alike. However, habits are hard to break and Mrs. Jackson and Mrs. Johnson found ten differences in the two houses. When the two ladies pointed out the differences to Mr. Jones, he just shook his head and said, "Oh, well, I never wanted to build two houses exactly alike, anyway!"

Find and **circle** ten differences in the families' houses.

Add three more details to both houses that are exactly **alike** and three more details that are **different**.

Name:

Date:

Demonstrating Visual Discrimination

Language Literacy Lessons / Reading Elementary
Copyright ©2002 by Incentive Publications, Inc.
Nashville, TN.

Birds in the Bush

The birds in the Bird World Park have gone into hiding.

Time yourself to find how quickly you can locate and circle 25 birds.

Record your time.

Five members of one bird family became separated during their frantic search for hiding places.

Find and color the five birds belonging to the same family.
(Hint: you will need to use your blue crayon.)

Add a safely hidden nest to the picture for the bird family.

Name: _____

Date: _____

Language Literacy Lessons / Reading Elementary
Copyright ©2002 by Incentive Publications, Inc.
Nashville, TN.

Demonstrating Visual Discrimination

Supply the E

Bonita needs help finishing her homework. She needs to change all her short-vowel words to make long-vowel words.

Read the directions to help Bonita finish her homework.

Add an E to each short-vowel word to make it a long-vowel word.

Not _____	Bit _____	Mat _____
Mad _____	Hop _____	Pan _____
Hug _____	Cub _____	Pin _____
Us _____	Hid _____	Can _____
Cap _____	At _____	Fin _____
Tub _____	Cut _____	Fat _____

Select one of the word pairs to use in sentences.

Write one sentence using the short-vowel word and one sentence using the long vowel word.

_____

_____

_____

_____

Name: _____ Date: _____

Short and Long Vowels

Language Literacy Lessons / Reading Elementary
Copyright ©2002 by Incentive Publications, Inc.
Nashville, TN.

Alphabet Antics

Amo and Anita had planned this trip to the amusement park for days. Who would have expected a rainstorm?

"Well," they said to each other, "every cloud has a silver lining. We won't let a little rain spoil our day. We'll play a game to pass the time away."

To amuse themselves they made up a game they named Alphabet Antics.

To join in their game, draw a line from an object in the picture to the beginning letter of the object's name.

Language Literacy Lessons / Reading Elementary
Copyright ©2002 by Incentive Publications, Inc.
Nashville, TN.

Beginning Sounds

Pick a Picture

Look at the pictures in the boxes.

Circle any picture whose name does not start with the letter in that box.

Color the other pictures.

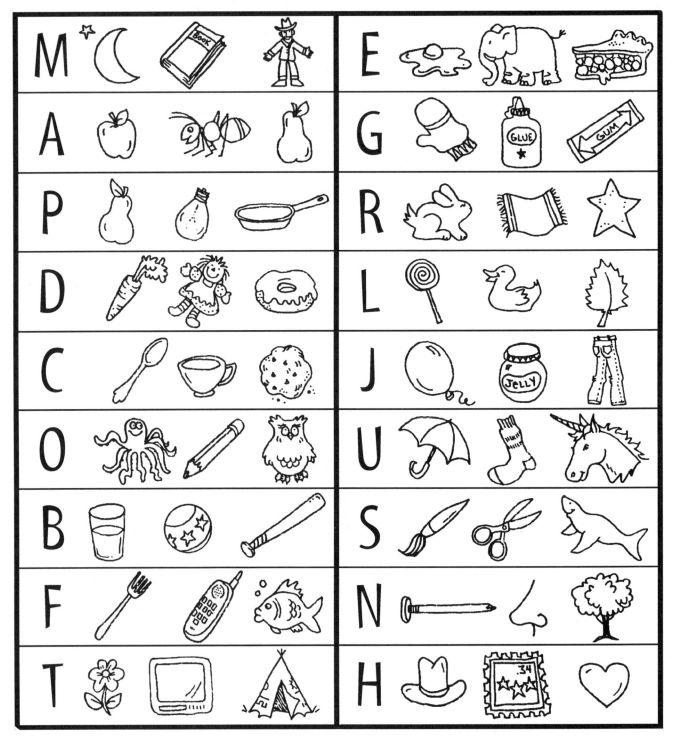

Name:

Date:

Beginning Sounds

Language Literacy Lessons / Reading Elementary
Copyright ©2002 by Incentive Publications, Inc.
Nashville, TN.

A Splendid Spider Web

Spunky Spider is spinning a special spider web.

This splendid web is filled with words beginning with the consonant blend **"sp."**

Find and circle 21 words in the word-find box.
Words appear up and down or across.

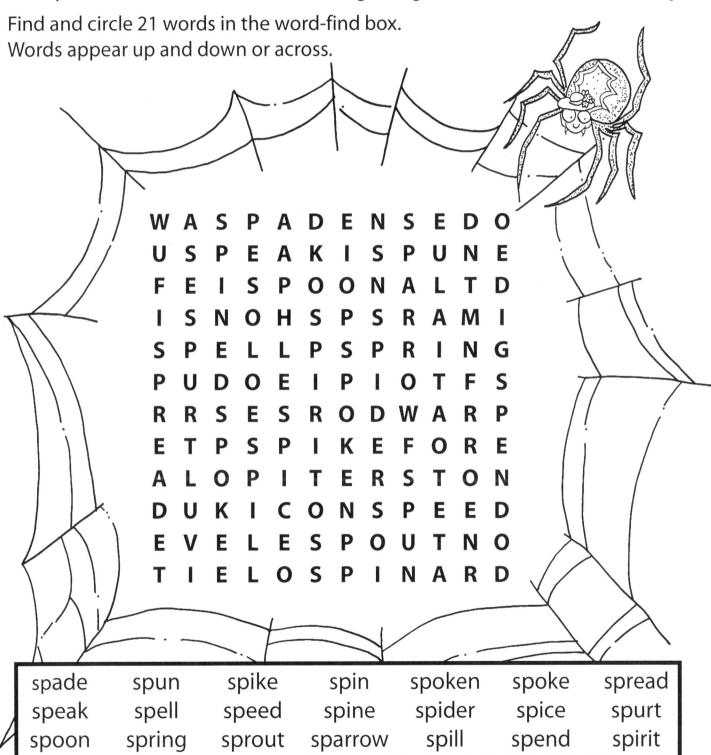

```
W  A  S  P  A  D  E  N  S  E  D  O
U  S  P  E  A  K  I  S  P  U  N  E
F  E  I  S  P  O  O  N  A  L  T  D
I  S  N  O  H  S  P  S  R  A  M  I
S  P  E  L  L  P  S  P  R  I  N  G
P  U  D  O  E  I  P  I  O  T  F  S
R  R  S  E  S  R  O  D  W  A  R  P
E  T  P  S  P  I  K  E  F  O  R  E
A  L  O  P  I  T  E  R  S  T  O  N
D  U  K  I  C  O  N  S  P  E  E  D
E  V  E  L  E  S  P  O  U  T  N  O
T  I  E  L  O  S  P  I  N  A  R  D
```

spade	spun	spike	spin	spoken	spoke	spread
speak	spell	speed	spine	spider	spice	spurt
spoon	spring	sprout	sparrow	spill	spend	spirit

Name: _____   Date: _____   ⑰

Copyright ©2002 by Incentive Publications, Inc.
Nashville, TN.

Using Consonant Blends

Sly Blends

Circle nine things in this picture that begin with the consonant blend *"gr."*

Underline nine things in this picture that begin with the consonant blend *"st."*

Add pictures of 2 things that begin with the consonant blend *"tr."*

Name:

Date:

Knows and Uses Consonant Blends

Language Literacy Lessons / Reading Elementary
Copyright ©2002 by Incentive Publications, Inc.
Nashville, TN.

A Funny Phonics Flower Garden

Color all the **consonant** spaces purple.

Color all the **vowel** spaces red.

How many funny phonics flowers did you color? _____

Name: _____   Date: _____

Language Literacy Lessons / Reading Elementary
Copyright ©2002 by Incentive Publications, Inc.
Nashville, TN.

Knows and Can Use Phonics

Rhyme Find

Finish these rhymes.

He is a better cook
when he uses the

_____ .

He put a guitar
in the trunk of his

_____ .

The big brown dog
is sitting on the

_____ .

Please ring the

_____

if you find a shell.

He took the fan
and away he

_____ .

I wish that I
could touch the

_____ .

My sister's

_____

is awfully fat!

If you don't want to hike,
you may ride your

_____ .

Name: _____   Date: _____

Recognizing Rhyming Words

Language Literacy Lessons / Reading Elementary
Copyright ©2002 by Incentive Publications, Inc.
Nashville, TN.

Rhymes on the Line

Put a word on the line
To make your own rhyme!

There once was a man
whose house was a
_____ .

The poor little bug
got caught in a
_____ .

Old Freddie the frog
just likes to
_____ .

One night in a tree
all the owls drank
_____ .

I got a phone call from a hen
who talked to me 'til almost
_____ .

Jack's the only crow I know
who likes to stand out in the
_____ .

Language Literacy Lessons / Reading Elementary
Copyright ©2002 by Incentive Publications, Inc.
Nashville, TN.

Recognizing Rhyming Words

Star Light, Star Bright

To solve the puzzle and find the hidden picture, read the phrases below and follow the directions.

1. If **clock** rhymes with **block**, color the #1 spaces.

2. If **star** rhymes with **bar**, color the #2 spaces.

3. If **sky** rhymes with **shed**, color the #3 spaces.

4. If **night** rhymes with **nine**, color the #4 spaces.

5. If **mid** rhymes with **map**, color the #5 spaces.

6. If **moon** rhymes with **spoon**, color the #6 spaces.

7. If **bright** rhymes with **fright**, color the #7 spaces.

8. If **dark** rhymes with **look**, color the #8 spaces.

9. If **cloud** rhymes with **count**, color the #9 spaces.

Name: _____   Date: _____

Recognizing Rhyming Words

Language Literacy Lessons / Reading Elementary
Copyright ©2002 by Incentive Publications, Inc.
Nashville, TN.

Mystery Mountain

A storm on Mystery Mountain has scrambled up the syllables in these words.
Rearrange the syllables correctly to find out what the sentences say.

1. chael-Mi _____

2. the _____

3. cian-gi-Ma _____

4. thinks _____

5. tains-moun _____

6. are _____

7. gic-ma _____

8. It's _____

9. ing-cit-ex

_____

10. to

_____

11. gaze

_____

12. to-in

_____

13. the

_____

14. ley-val

_____

15. low-be

_____

Add three sentences of your own
to tell more about Mystery Mountain.

_____

_____

_____

_____

_____

_____

Name: _____ Date: _____ 23

Using Rules for Syllabication

Magician's Makeover

Michael the Magician is busy "making over" words by adding suffixes to root words to form new words.

Draw a line from each suffix on the right to a word on the left to make a new word.

Say the new words aloud.

quiet   -able

kind   -ish

fool   -er

wash   -ful

allow   -ness

grace   -ly

loud   -ance

Name: _____   Date: _____

Using Suffixes

Language Literacy Lessons / Reading Elementary
Copyright ©2002 by Incentive Publications, Inc.
Nashville, TN.

Prefix Go-Round

Draw a line from each prefix on the Prefix Wheel to a word in the center of the wheel to make new words.

Say the new words aloud.

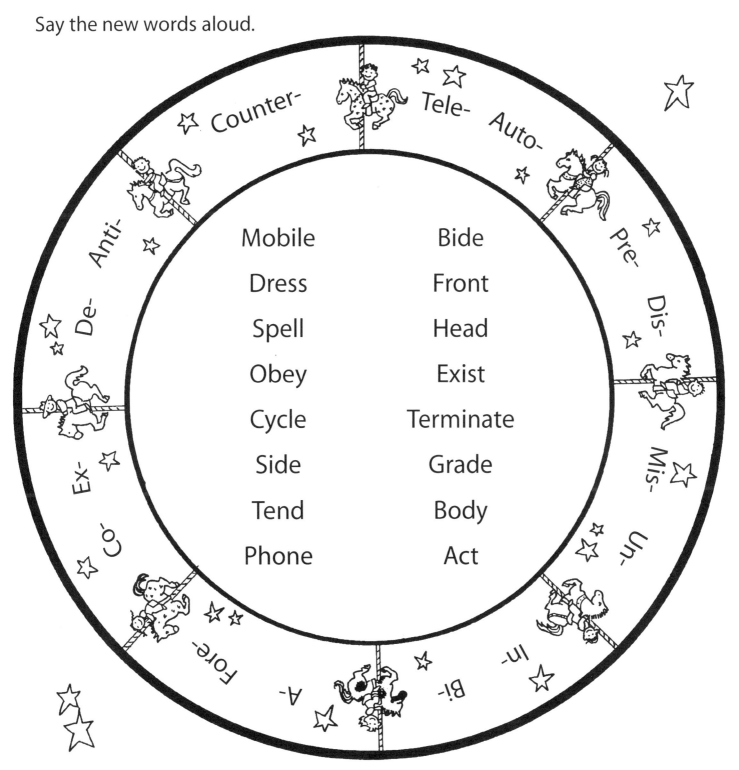

Language Literacy Lessons / Reading Elementary
Copyright ©2002 by Incentive Publications, Inc.
Nashville, TN.

Using Prefixes and Suffixes

Contraction Action

A contraction is formed when two words are joined together with an apostrophe in the middle.

Find contractions in the contraction corral to complete each sentence below.

You _____ want to miss the big Rodeo Roundup. _____ scheduled to begin promptly at 8:00 p.m. tomorrow if it _____ raining. If the sun _____ shine, the show _____ go on. The rodeo _____ start until all the horses are in place.

_____ want to see a rodeo without horses? The cowboys _____ be very interesting without horses, would they? They _____ move very fast or create much excitement.

_____ just something about horses that makes a rodeo worth seeing.

Remember, _____ start promptly at eight.

For a thrill _____ never forget, you _____ be late.

don't   shouldn't

it's   doesn't

isn't   there's

won't   they'll

can't   you'll

who'd   mustn't

wouldn't

Name: _____   Date: _____

Using Contractions

Language Literacy Lessons / Reading Elementary
Copyright ©2002 by Incentive Publications, Inc.
Nashville, TN.

Compound Top

Round and round goes the Compound Top!
Circle the words to make it stop!

Find and circle 14 compound words on the top.

Say the compound words aloud.

classroom
goldfish
football   airplane
popcorn   butterfly
houseboat   eggshell
cowboy   outside
carport   tentmaker
highway   doorbell

Name: Date:

Language Literacy Lessons / Reading Elementary   Using Compound Words
Copyright ©2002 by Incentive Publications, Inc.
Nashville, TN.

Pick the Plurals

"Pick" the flower in each group that shows more than one object.

Color flowers yellow that do not show plurals.

Color flowers red if they are plurals.

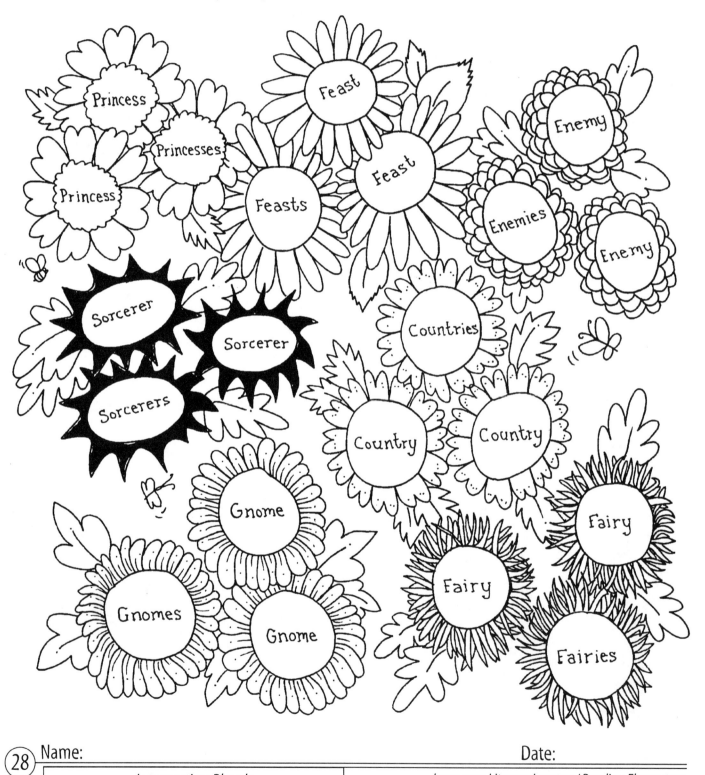

Name: _____   Date: _____

Interpreting Plurals   *Language Literacy Lessons / Reading Elementary*
Copyright ©2002 by Incentive Publications, Inc.
Nashville, TN.

Two of Everything

The Caver twins' mother is packing their suitcases.
They are going to visit their grandmother.
Since there are two babies, they will need two of everything.

Help their mother pack the car by writing the plural beside each item.

buggy . . . .

diaper . . . .

baby wipe

blanket . . . .

suit . . . .

shirt . . . .

hat . . . .

pillow . . . .

rattle . . . .

bunny . . . .

bib . . . .

pacifier . . . .

bottle . . . .

Name: _____   Date: _____

Language Literacy Lessons / Reading Elementary
Copyright ©2002 by Incentive Publications, Inc.
Nashville, TN.

Plurals

The Leprechaun's Music Box

There are 13 words hiding in the leprechaun's music box.
Read the list of words. Then find and circle them in the music box.
Words appear down, across and diagonal, but never backwards.

Words to find:

Band	Drum	Jazz	Radio
Beat	Guitar	Melody	Rhythm
Clap	Hum	Notes	Singer
			Song

Name:

Date:

Sight Vocabulary

Language Literacy Lessons / Reading Elementary
Copyright ©2002 by Incentive Publications, Inc.
Nashville, TN.

Family Fun

Write a word to finish each sentence below.
Figure out what words you need
by looking at this picture.

1. _____mother is reading to Joey.

2. Mother is pushing the lawn_____ .

3. Father is hanging wet towels on the clothes_____ .

4. Ethel and Arnold are tossing a base_____ .

5. Grand_____ is bringing lemonade for everyone.

6. Baby is _____ soundly.

7. Sue is reading a _____ .

8. The _____ is buzzing about.

9. It is a bright, _____ day.

10. Katrina loves to hear Grandmother _____ .

Words to use:
sunny
bee
book
sleeping
read
father
line
ball
Grand
mower

Name: _____   Date: _____   31

King Wiseapple's Rebus

Old King Wiseapple's wizard got stuck in one of his own magic spells and disappeared before he could solve these two rebuses. Can you help King Wiseapple out by solving the rebuses?

Look at the rebus boxes, and figure them out. Write your solutions on the line below each rebus block.

1.

2.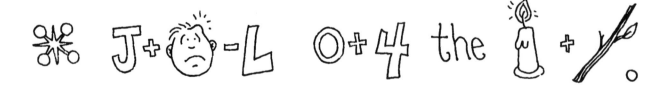

Name: _____

Date: _____

Rebuses

Language Literacy Lessons / Reading Elementary
Copyright ©2002 by Incentive Publications, Inc.
Nashville, TN.

The Dwarf's Story

Read the story below and circle the proper word
to fit each blank.

Rain was falling as the (twisted, ugly) little dwarf hurried down the narrow street as (quickly, poor) as his (spindly, brave) legs would carry him. He moved (quietly, loudly) from doorway to doorway, hoping he would not be (secret, noticed). Under the plain brown cloak that covered his (planted, twisted) little body, he carried a (secret, happy) bundle of great value.

At last he came to the cottage of a (loud, poor) farmer just outside the village. He very carefully laid the bundle on the doorstep, rapped (loudly, spindly) on the door, and hurried away before he could be seen.

When the farmer and his wife opened the door, they saw only the bundle lying on the step. Seeing what it was, the woman snatched it up and cried with tears of (joy, sadness), "Oh, blessings on the kind and (brave, guilty) soul who has rescued our (beautiful, large) baby from the castle of the wicked queen. Surely the queen was jealous of the beauty of our child and took him for her own. Whoever has returned him to us is a noble person indeed!"

Name: Date:

Language Literacy Lessons / Reading Elementary
Copyright ©2002 by Incentive Publications, Inc.
Nashville, TN.

Context Clues

Pack the Basket

Hooray! Today is Picnic Day.

Help pack the picnic basket.
Mark out the item in each group that does not belong at a picnic.

Draw one thing in the basket that you would like to have at a picnic.

Name: _____

Date: _____

Word Classification

Hot Dog Hang-Up

Poor Mr. Giorgio! He is setting up a hot dog stand for the county fair. He has a problem organizing equipment and supplies.

Help him decide what goes where by labeling the food with a big **F**, and all the cooking equipment with a big **E**.

Then on another sheet write out a menu for Mr. Giorgio's hot dog stand.

Name:

Date:

Language Literacy Lessons / Reading Elementary
Copyright ©2002 by Incentive Publications, Inc.
Nashville, TN.

Word Classification

Royal Words

In each group below, cross out the word that does not belong.

Write a sentence explaining why it does not belong.

KING QUEEN NURSE

PRINCE PUPPY PRINCESS

PAN JEWEL CROWN

PALACE BARN CASTLE

Name:

Date:

Word Classification

Language Literacy Lessons / Reading Elementary
Copyright ©2002 by Incentive Publications, Inc.
Nashville, TN.

Homonym Homework

Help Homonym Homer finish his homework.

Write the correct homonym in the space beside each word.
(You will find all the homonyms hiding in the backpack!)

HOUR

MEAT

IN

SORE

SCENTS

RODE

WON

READ

AUNT

PLAIN

ONE

MEET   ROAD

OUR

SOAR   CENTS

INN

RED   ANT   PLANE

Name:

Date:

Language Literacy Lessons / Reading Elementary
Copyright ©2002 by Incentive Publications, Inc.
Nashville, TN.

Homonyms

Picture the Meaning

Draw a picture to illustrate the meaning of each saying below.

A bird in the hand is worth two in the bush.	He's in a pretty pickle.
I was shaking in my boots.	A penny saved is a penny earned.

Name:

Date:

Interpreting and Conveying Meanings of a Variety of Familiar Words

Language Literacy Lessons / Reading Elementary
Copyright ©2002 by Incentive Publications, Inc.
Nashville, TN.

Off to Battle

Look at the picture carefully.
Select a word from the list to finish each sentence.

1. The soldiers' path is rocky and _____ .

2. Even the big bird looks _____ .

3. The _____ troll is falling behind.

4. The second soldier looks _____ than the other two.

5. The tallest soldier's hat is on _____ .

6. The flag is being carried _____ into battle.

7. These soldiers need to be very _____ .

8. The dog looks _____ .

9. The dark sky is _____ .

Words to use:
angry
rugged
proudly
vicious
backwards
friendlier
brave
frightening
grouchy

Name: Date:

Language Literacy Lessons / Reading Elementary
Copyright ©2002 by Incentive Publications, Inc.
Nashville, TN.

Word Relationships

Goblins and Hobgoblins

Fill each blank below with the best descriptive word from the word list.

1. Goblins are said to be bad-hearted and _____ creatures.

2. Goblins are pictured as little, ugly, and _____ .

3. It is said that goblins like to torment and _____ victims.

4. Meeting a goblin would be a _____ experience for most people.

5. Hobgoblins are said to be _____ spirits who do only mischievous deeds.

6. Hobgoblins are _____ little creatures who like to play tricks on people.

7. Getting acquainted with a hobgoblin might be _____ and _____ .

8. Goblins are actually only _____ creatures.

Write two sentences describing a happy goblin.

9. _____

10. _____

Words to use:

troublesome	frighten	imaginative	harmless
friendly	exciting	interesting	terrifying
			mean

Name: _____   Date: _____

Using Descriptive Words

Language Literacy Lessons / Reading Elementary
Copyright ©2002 by Incentive Publications, Inc.
Nashville, TN.

Which is What?

Look carefully at the four make-believe characters below.
On the lines next to each picture, write the four words from the word list which best describe that character.

Add one descriptive word of your own to each word list.

Words to use:

beautiful   noble   strong

enchanting   playful   dainty

imaginative   quick   delicate

brave

disciplined   fearless   majestic

courageous   tiny   harmless

Name: _____   Date: _____

Language Literacy Lessons / Reading Elementary
Copyright ©2002 by Incentive Publications, Inc.
Nashville, TN.

Descriptive Words

A Bag of Words

Use your dictionary if you need help to find at least 15 words to describe this creature.

Use some of the words to write a sentence telling something you think the creature could do.

1. _____
2. _____
3. _____
4. _____
5. _____
6. _____
7. _____
8. _____

9. _____
10. _____
11. _____
12. _____
13. _____
14. _____
15. _____

_____

_____

Name: _____   Date: _____

Descriptive Words

Language Literacy Lessons / Reading Elementary
Copyright ©2002 by Incentive Publications, Inc.
Nashville, TN.

Comprehension and Independent Reading Skills

Flying High!

Put the number of the bird beside the sentence that you think best describes that bird's feelings.

_____ I wonder if I could fly that high.   _____ It's a long way down.

_____ A mother's work is never done.   _____ Why leave the nest now?

Then choose one of the four birds to write a story about. Use the sentence you selected to describe that bird's feelings as the title of your story. Write your story on the back of the page.

Name: _____   Date: _____

Associating Words with Feelings

Language Literacy Lessons / Reading Elementary
Copyright ©2002 by Incentive Publications, Inc.
Nashville, TN.

What Does it Look Like?

Sometimes when you say a word, you can see exactly what you think it looks like in your mind. For instance, when you say the word "pumpkin," you might see it like this.

Read the following words. Draw a picture of each as you "see" it in your mind.

slipper	cake
heart	rainbow
crown	carriage

Name:

Date:

Sensory Impressions

In the Middle of the Night

Imagine that you awoke in the middle of a cold and rainy night to find all the characters from your favorite fairy tale dancing around your room.

Draw a picture here to show the scene.

Name:

Date:

Sensory Impressions

Language Literacy Lessons / Reading Elementary
Copyright ©2002 by Incentive Publications, Inc.
Nashville, TN.

Through an Open Window

Look through this window.

How do you know that it is Mother's birthday? _____

_____

How old is Mother? _____ How did you figure this out? _____

_____

How do you know what the weather is like outside?_____

_____

How many generations are represented at this party? _____

What is the family hobby? _____

How did you figure this out? _____

_____

Name: _____ Date: _____ 47

Picture and Idea Association

Elves in the Picture

Study this picture for a few minutes.

Then, cover the picture with a sheet of paper.

Complete the sentences below.
Then uncover the picture to check your answers.

1. There are _____ elves in the picture.

2. There are _____ glasses on the table.

3. There are _____ chairs in the picture.

4. The table is set for _____ people.

5. The basket is filled with _____ .

6. The smallest elf has a _____ on his hat.

7. One elf is holding a knife in her hand; another is holding a _____ .

8. A good title for this picture would be

_____

Name: _____

Date: _____

*Recalling Information Read
and Selecting Facts to Remember*

Language Literacy Lessons / Reading Elementary
Copyright ©2002 by Incentive Publications, Inc.
Nashville, TN.

A Fruitful Memory

Look carefully at this picture for just 2 minutes.
Then cover the picture with a clean sheet of paper.
Write the names of as many fruits as you can remember on the paper.
Try for 11 different fruits.

Now, draw a picture of each fruit beside its name.
Then, return to this page and see how many fruits you can draw in the picture
that are not already represented.

Name: _____

Date: _____

Language Literacy Lessons / Reading Elementary
Copyright ©2002 by Incentive Publications, Inc.
Nashville, TN.

Remembering Details from Pictures

It's A Fact!

Some of the sentences below state **facts**. That means they are true.

Some of the sentences state **opinions**. That means they are what someone thinks, and are not necessarily true.

Circle the sentences that state facts.
Underline the sentences that state opinions.

...the facts...

1. Roberto is sure to win the race tomorrow.

2. There are at least 9 planets in our solar system.

3. The month of January has 31 days.

4. Chickens hatch from eggs.

5. I think I hear footsteps outside my window.

6. Angela is the best skater in town.

7. Monster stories are the best stories to read.

8. There are 7 days in a week.

9. Swimming is more fun than any other sport.

10. A period goes at the end of a "telling" sentence.

11. Sammy says ice cream has just as much food value as broccoli.

12. A beach vacation is more fun than a skiing trip.

13. Twelve eggs make one dozen.

14. Mary Ann's report on Asia was better than Ken's.

...my opinion...

Name: _____

Date: _____

Distinguishing Between Fact and Opinion

Language Literacy Lessons / Reading Elementary
Copyright ©2002 by Incentive Publications, Inc.
Nashville, TN.

After Mother Goose

Underline each word in the Mother Goose rhymes that tells what the main character did.

Draw a picture to show what you think happened next.

Old King Cole
Was a merry old soul,
And a merry old soul
    was he.
He called for his pipe,
And he called for his bowl,
And he called for his fiddlers three!

Little Miss Muffet
Sat on a tuffet
Eating her curds
    and whey.
Along came a spider
And sat down beside her
And frightened Miss Muffet away.

Little Jack Horner
Sat in a corner,
Eating a Christmas pie.
He stuck in
    his thumb
And pulled out
    a plum,
And said, "What a good boy am I!"

Name:

Date:

Language Literacy Lessons / Reading Elementary
Copyright ©2002 by Incentive Publications, Inc.
Nashville, TN.

Finding the Main Idea

Kahlil the Shepherd

Read the story below.

Underline the topic sentence in each paragraph.

Late one afternoon, Kahlil the Shepherd sat watching his flock. It was his job to care for the sheep of the village. Each day, he would take the flock out to graze. Each day, he and his faithful dog Ali would look after them, keeping the wolves away and helping the little lambs that got caught in the bushes. Today they had been very busy, and now everything was quiet and calm.

Suddenly, Ali started to bark and growl. Kahlil jumped up and looked around to see what had made Ali excited. He saw nothing, but he heard a "clip, clop, clip, clop." It sounded like a horse coming slowly up the road. He looked down the path and saw an old man walking, leading a tired donkey behind him. The old man looked so sad and the donkey so thin that Kahlil felt sorry for them.

When they reached Kahlil, he nodded and said, "Old man, you look tired and hungry, and so does your donkey. Stop here, and rest for a moment. I'll share my bread and cheese with you, and your donkey may graze with my sheep, if you will tell me the tale of your journey. I have never left this village, and I would like to hear about the wide world. Your looks say you have seen much of it."

Name: _____

Date: _____

Identifying Topic Sentences

Language Literacy Lessons / Reading Elementary
Copyright ©2002 by Incentive Publications, Inc.
Nashville, TN.

A Spring Storm

Ilene and her family were taking a driving trip across the country. As they drove one day, Ilene asked her mom to turn on the radio. Just as her mom tuned in a station, this newscast came on.

This is station WKZR in Bean Blossom. Our newsroom has just received information that a freak spring snowstorm is moving into our territory from the northwest at 37 miles per hour, and should reach Bean Blossom within an hour. All schools and daycare centers are sending their students home now before the storm hits. All businesses are closing. High winds of up to 45 miles per hour, blowing snow, and sleet will accompany the storm, causing limited visibility and bad driving conditions.

The storm is expected to last until noon tomorrow. Stay tuned to station WKZR in Bean Blossom for further information on the storm as it develops. In the meantime, get home and stay warm!

Underline only the most important facts in the above newscast. Then, using only the facts, rewrite the bulletin in as few words as possible.

_____

_____

_____

_____

_____

_____

_____

_____

_____

Name: _____   Date: _____   (53)

Reading to Find Details

Far-Out Facts

Read this ad from the Galaxia Gazette, then answer the questions below.

At last, hair that is
OUT OF THIS WORLD!!!

If you have wanted to try the new "Solar-shock" look that is sweeping the galaxy, **MOONDRIPS** shampoo is just for you! Even fine, limp hair can be made to stand on end with this wonderful shampoo. Made with tiny bits of magnet, **MOONDRIPS** will keep your new hairdo charged with life for days!

Only $3.95 per bottle.

MOONDRIPS
SHAMPOO

Sold only at the
Star-Struck Store.

1. What is the ad trying to sell? _____

2. What is this product made from that makes it special? _____

3. What new look is sweeping the galaxy?_____

4. In what store can it be found? _____

5. How much does the product cost? _____

Name: _____   Date: _____

Reading to Find Details

Language Literacy Lessons / Reading Elementary
Copyright ©2002 by Incentive Publications, Inc.
Nashville, TN.

What Goes When?

This comic strip
is out of order.

Look at each frame carefully.

Write the correct number
(1–4) on each frame to put
the cartoon in the right order.

On the lines below, write a
story to accompany
the frames.

Color the pictures.

_____

_____

_____

_____

_____

_____

_____

_____

_____

_____

_____

_____

Name: _____   Date: _____

Language Literacy Lessons / Reading Elementary
Copyright ©2002 by Incentive Publications, Inc.
Nashville, TN.

Arranging Ideas or Events in Sequence

Royal Conclusions

Finish the following diagrams by drawing picture conclusions in the spaces provided.

Name:

Date:

Drawing Conclusions

Language Literacy Lessons / Reading Elementary
Copyright ©2002 by Incentive Publications, Inc.
Nashville, TN.

Change the Story

All summer long, the grasshopper danced and sang in the warm sunshine. When winter came and the earth was bare, he had nothing to eat.

One cold day, the hungry grasshopper saw an ant happily eating dinner. "Where did you get that lovely food?" he asked.

"Oh," said the ant, "I always store food in the summer so I will have something to eat in the winter."

"Will you please give me just enough to keep me from starving?" begged the grasshopper.

"No, I won't," said the ant. "You danced and sang all summer while I worked. Now you can just dance and sing all winter!"

Write what you think would have happened if . . .

1. The ant had kindly invited the grasshopper for some food.

_____

_____

_____

_____

2. The grasshopper had been a thief and had tried to rob the ant.

_____

_____

_____

_____

Language Literacy Lessons / Reading Elementary
Copyright ©2002 by Incentive Publications, Inc.
Nashville, TN.

Drawing Conclusions

Concluding Conclusions

Finish the following diagrams by "reading" them and drawing picture conclusions in the spaces provided.

Name:

Date:

Drawing Conclusions

Language Literacy Lessons / Reading Elementary
Copyright ©2002 by Incentive Publications, Inc.
Nashville, TN.

The Other Side of It

Write the other half of each conversation in the correct balloon.

Language Literacy Lessons / Reading Elementary
Copyright ©2002 by Incentive Publications, Inc.
Nashville, TN.

Distinguishing Between Cause and Effect

Just Because

The pictures in eight of these circles show something that happened.
Each picture in the other eight circles shows an effect of one of the happenings.

Draw lines to connect each "cause" circle with its correct "effect" circle.

Select one "cause-and-effect" circle set to use as the theme for a creative story.

Name: _____   Date: _____

Distinguishing Between Cause and Effect

Language Literacy Lessons / Reading Elementary
Copyright ©2002 by Incentive Publications, Inc.
Nashville, TN.

Oops! Wrong Page!

Cross out the words that do not belong on each dictionary page.

Use the guidewords to help you decide which words *do not* fit.

Add two more words to each group that *do* fit on each dictionary page.

cow   cut

come   cub
crab   chair
creek   curl
crow   curly
crown   cut

leg   live

lemon   limp
let   lap
lie   line
light   list
laugh   love

men   mouse

mess   miss
milk   mix
mad   meat
mat   mop
mile   mother

pat   puppy

paw   pizza
pen   plane
pet   dog
pick   play
bat   pool

seal   soon   hello   hurry

see   sick   hen   hog
set   sat   hide   hop
shark   sister   he   hot
chip   sleep   hill   hug
ship   snake   hat   hurt

Name:

Date:

Using the Dictionary

A B C Bakery

Help Mr. Edwards arrange his new bakery.
Place the items on the shelves in alphabetical order by
writing them in the correct place on the lines below each shelf.

Muffins: bran; corn; blueberry
Doughnuts: maple; cream-filled; jelly
Pies: pecan; pumpkin; apple

Cakes: carrot; devil's food; coconut
Cookies: peanut butter; sugar; chocolate chip
Bread: rye; wheat; raisin

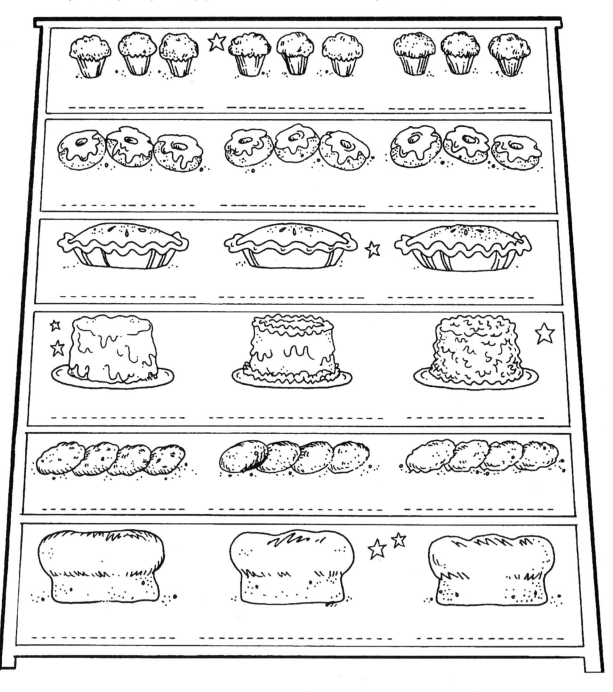

Name: _____

Date: _____

Alphabetical Order

A Marsupial Puzzle

Do you know what **marsupial** means?

It is the name of a very special group of animals that have pouches to carry their young and are usually found in Australia.
The koala is one kind of marsupial.

To discover the koala in hiding, cut out the squares on the bottom half of this page. Put them together so that they show this cuddly animal curled fast asleep in a eucalyptus tree. Paste the squares in the correct spaces on a blank page. Color your finished puzzle. Then find a book to help you learn more about this and other marsupials that live in Australia.

Name: _____

Date: _____

Language Literacy Lessons / Reading Elementary
Copyright ©2002 by Incentive Publications, Inc.
Nashville, TN.

Using Reference Sources and Multiple Resources

Punctuation Pointers

Point out what you know!

Work the crossword puzzle to show your knowledge of punctuation skills.

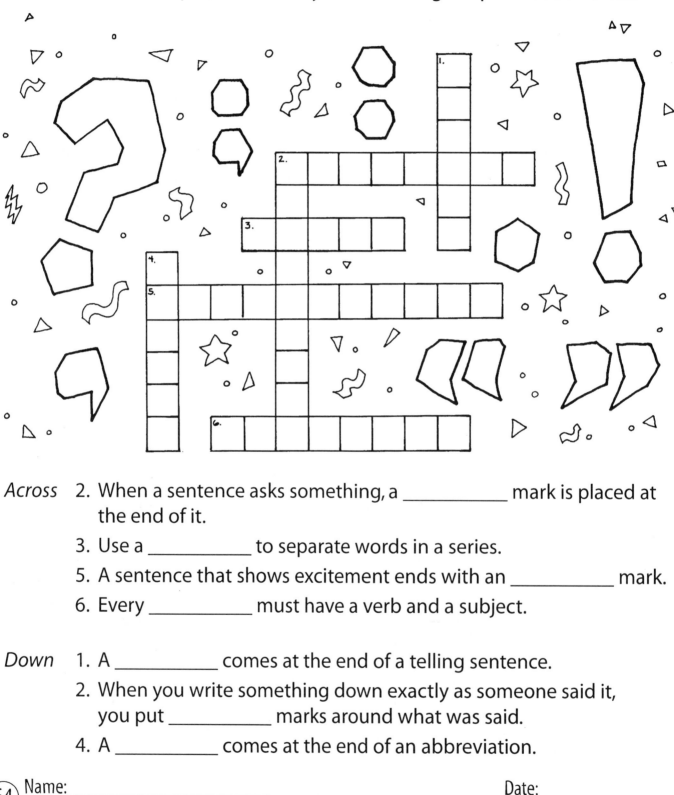

Across 2. When a sentence asks something, a _____ mark is placed at the end of it.

   3. Use a _____ to separate words in a series.

   5. A sentence that shows excitement ends with an _____ mark.

   6. Every _____ must have a verb and a subject.

Down 1. A _____ comes at the end of a telling sentence.

   2. When you write something down exactly as someone said it, you put _____ marks around what was said.

   4. A _____ comes at the end of an abbreviation.

Name: _____   Date: _____

Understanding and Using Punctuation   *Language Literacy Lessons / Reading Elementary*
Copyright ©2002 by Incentive Publications, Inc.
Nashville, TN.

A Plain Paper Plane Plan

Marla was just learning to speak English.
Joe made this plan for her to follow to make a paper plane.

See if you can follow the diagram to make a paper airplane.
When you have finished, decorate your airplane and send
it for a spin.

Name: _____   Date: _____

Language Literacy Lessons / Reading Elementary
Copyright ©2002 by Incentive Publications, Inc.
Nashville, TN.

Following Directions

Fruit Salad

Follow these directions to complete the "Fruit Salad" poster.
You will need a pencil and some crayons.

1. Write your name under the basket.
2. Draw another leaf on the stem of the apple.
3. Color the apple red, and the stem of the leaves green.
4. Write the names of three fruits besides **pear** that begin with the letter "p."
5. Give the pear a smiling face.
6. Use your pencil to add enough grapes to make an even dozen.
7. Write four words on the banana describing how it would taste.
8. Draw a handle on the basket.
9. Use your favorite crayon to draw a big bow on the handle.
10. Color all of the fruits.
11. Write a recipe for fruit salad on the back of the sheet.

Name: _____   Date: _____

Following Directions

Language Literacy Lessons / Reading Elementary
Copyright ©2002 by INCENTIVE PUBLICATIONS, Inc.
Nashville, TN.

After the Rain

Use red, green, yellow, purple, gold, and blue to color this picture—a secret just for you!

Color the #1 spaces red.

Color the #2 spaces green.

Color the #3 spaces yellow.

Color the #4 spaces purple.

Color the #5 spaces blue.

Color the #6 spaces orange.

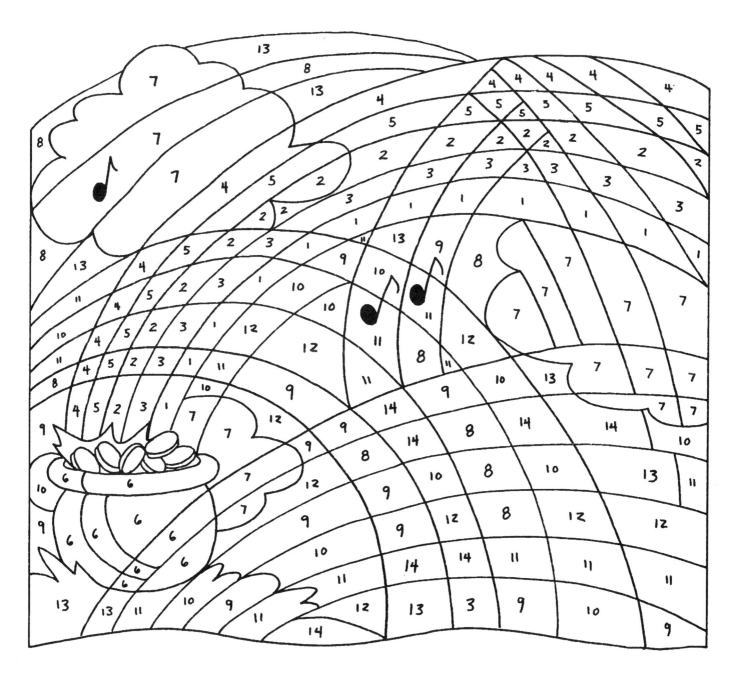

Name: _____

Date: _____

Following Directions

Jewelry Fit for a Queen

The chief designer for the Queen's jewelry factory had a bad day.

The instructions for making lovely jewelry are mixed up.

Read all the instructions, and then number them in the correct order in which they **should** be followed.

What to use:

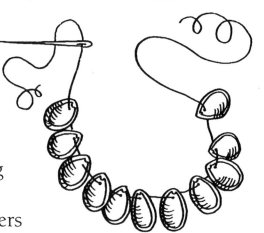

water
needle
thread
pumpkin seeds
red and green food coloring
2 small jars with tops
paper towels and/or newspapers

_____ Thread your needle, and make a knot at the end of the thread.

_____ Spread the seeds on paper to dry.

_____ Add $\frac{1}{2}$ teaspoon of water to each jar.

_____ Put some seeds in each of 2 jars. Put a little red food coloring in one jar, a little green food coloring in the other jar.

_____ Shake the jars until the seeds are colored.

_____ Wash the pumpkin seeds and dry them on paper towels.

_____ String the seeds in several lengths to make the Queen's jewelry.
You can make original, one-of-a-kind rings, necklaces, or bracelets.

A Busy Barnyard

To understand the directions below, you must first figure out where one word stops and the next one begins. When you have done this, write the instructions in the space below. Follow them to complete the "Busy Barnyard."

Dra wamoun tainb ehi ndth eba rn. Addad ooran dtwowi ndowst otheb arn. Dra wtwoco wsaho rsean dsixc hick ensaro undth ebarn. Addth ree morean imals totheb arn yardsc ene.

_____

_____

_____

Name: _____   Date: _____

Language Literacy Lessons / Reading Elementary
Copyright ©2002 by Incentive Publications, Inc.
Nashville, TN.

Following Directions

Know Your Newspaper

Use a copy of today's newspaper to complete the sentences below.

Hometown News

VOL 30   ISSUE 40   75¢

THIS WEEK
☆ SPORTS
☆ COMMUNITY
☆ WANT ADS

1. The full name of the newspaper is

_____

_____ .

2. The newspaper is dated _____ .

3. The newspaper has _____ pages.

4. The most important article on the front page is about

_____

_____ .

5. The section of the newspaper that interests me most is

_____ .

Research an Animal

Select an animal that you would like to know more about.

Use two books from the library to help you learn more about this animal.

Make notes below and share your information with your teacher or parent.

Name of animal _____

Titles of books

1. _____

2. _____

Description of animal _____

_____

Where the animal lives _____

_____

How the animal looks _____

_____

What the animal eats _____

_____

Other interesting facts _____

_____

_____

_____

Name: _____   Date: _____ (71)

*Determining What Reference Source to Use, and
Using Multiple Resources*

Ari's Story

Read Ari's story.

Underline the three key sentences that tell what the story is about.

Circle the sentence that tells how Ari feels about the new school.

The select a good title for the story and write it on the title line.

_____

Ari found his first week in the school very interesting. One thing that made it so interesting was that this was also his first week to live in this new country. The days he spent in the boat at sea, the long trip on the train, and then the bus ride to this town were still fresh in his mind. The big brick building, with what seemed to be a million windows, was very different from his old school. His homeland seemed so far away. The palm trees, dates and lemons, and the tiny school he attended with his brothers were just memories. Yet so many things felt just the same. Even with this brand new language, Ari understood his classmates' offers to help. He understood the teacher's smiles and instructions about lessons and homework. On the playground, the games were different, but

the teammates laughs and slaps on the back when he kicked the balled, seemed just the same. In music class he was learning new songs, but the tunes sounded familiar. Best of all, these new friends seemed interested in learning about his old home and his old school. Ari thought this new school might be just fine after all.

Name:

Date:

Reading for Meaning

Language Literacy Lessons / Reading Elementary
Copyright ©2002 by Incentive Publications, Inc.
Nashville, TN.

Be A Word Bird

Just as birds are always searching for worms, good readers need to continually search for new and exciting words.

As you read this week, look for new words that you did not know before to add to your speaking, reading, and writing vocabulary.

Write these new words on the lines below.

_____   _____   _____

_____   _____   _____

_____   _____   _____

_____   _____   _____

_____   _____   _____

_____   _____   _____

_____   _____   _____

_____   _____   _____

_____   _____   _____

_____   _____   _____

_____   _____   _____

Name: _____   Date: _____

Language Literacy Lessons / Reading Elementary
Copyright ©2002 by Incentive Publications, Inc.
Nashville, TN.

Extending Vocabulary

A Letter to the Author

Select a book that you like. Write a letter to the author.

Tell the author the name of the book you have selected, what you like about the book, and how you would have changed it if you had been the author.

Share your letter with your teacher or librarian and ask for help in finding the author's mailing address. Send your letter!

Dear _____ ,

Sincerely,

Name: _____

Date: _____

Developing Reading Appreciation and Independence

Appendix

_____ 's Book Stack

Keep a record of your reading by writing titles of books as you read them.
Ask a friend to race with you to see whose book stack is finished first.

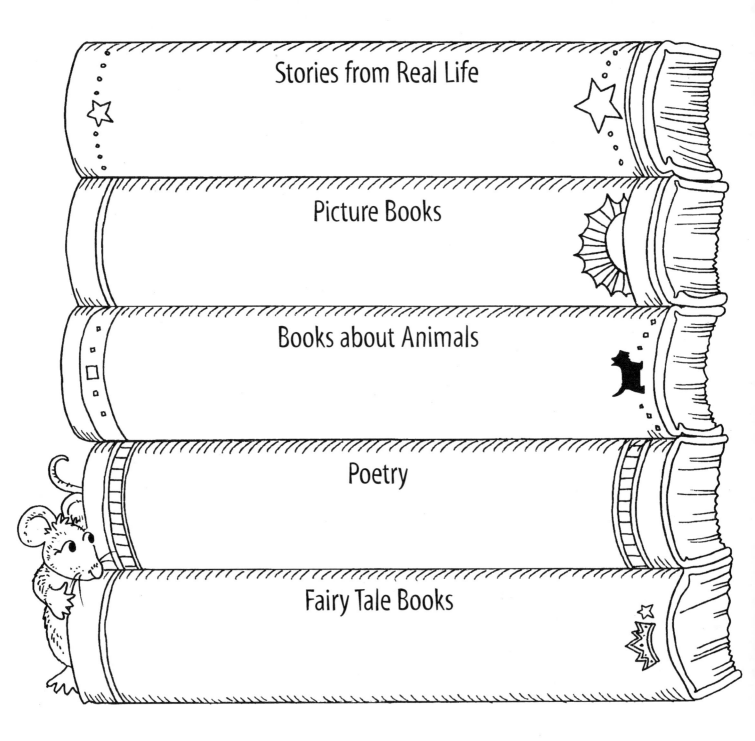

Stories from Real Life

Picture Books

Books about Animals

Poetry

Fairy Tale Books

Language Literacy Lessons / Reading Elementary
Copyright ©2002 by Incentive Publications, Inc.
Nashville, TN.

Answer Key

Page 12

Students should have found differences in the following:

1. windows
2. shingles
3. chimneys
4. doors
5. window in door
6. light/no light above door
7. siding on peak of house
8. brick vs. stone foundation
9. porch
10. trim on house

Page 16

The following should be circled:

Book	Glass	Duck
Pear	Phone	Balloon
Light bulb	Flower	Sock
Carrot	Pie	Paintbrush
Spoon	Mitten	Tree
Pencil	Star	Stamp

Page 17

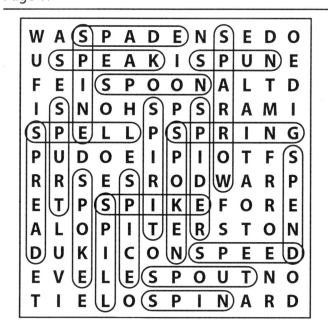

Page 18

Possible items circled (5 items should be circled):

Gramps'	Grapes
Grocery	Grapefruit
Grill	Grinning child
Growling dog	Graves
Word "grass" on sign	

Possible items underlined (4 items should be underlined) :

"Street" in sign	Stick
"stop" sign	Stump of tree
Striped shirt	"Store" sign
Steam off grill	Stork
Stones	

Check to be sure students added two items that begin with "tr-"

Page 19

Six flowers

Page 20

book	log	ran	cat
car	bell	sky	bike

Page 21

can	rug	jog	tea	ten	snow

Page 22

You are a ★!

Page 23

Michael the Magician thinks mountains are magic.
It's exciting to gaze into the valley below.

Page 24

quietly	allowance
kindness or kindly	graceful
foolish	louder or loudly
washer	

Answer Key

Page 25

Telephone	Inside	Degrade
Automobile	Bicycle	Counteract
Preexist	Abide	Antibody
Disobey	Forehead	Forefront
Misspell	Coexist	Exterminate
Undress	Extend	

Page 26

don't	wouldn't
It's	can't
isn't	There's
doesn't	they'll
won't	you'll
mustn't	shouldn't
Who'd	

Page 27

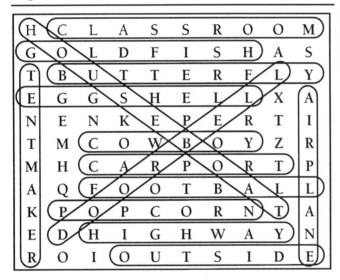

Page 28

Check to be sure students have correctly identified plurals.

Page 29

buggies	hats	bibs
diapers	pillows	pacifiers
baby wipes	shirts	bottles
blankets	rattles	
suits	bunnies	

Page 30

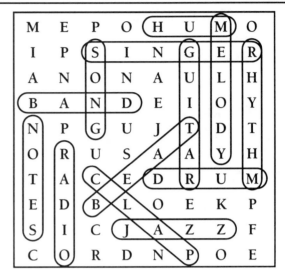

Page 31

1. Grand	6. sleeping
2. mower	7. book
3. line	8. bee
4. ball	9. sunny
5. mother	10. read

Page 32

1. Twinkle, twinkle, little star
   How I wonder what you are.
2. Jack be nimble, Jack be quick,
   Jack jumped over the candlestick.

Page 33

ugly	secret
quickly	poor
spindly	loudly
quietly	joy
noticed	brave
twisted	beautiful

Page 34

Items that do not belong:
   math book, mittens, light bulb, pencils, scissors, and hammer

Page 36

Words that do not belong: nurse, puppy, pan, barn
   Sentences will vary.

Language Literacy Lessons / Reading Elementary
Copyright ©2002 by Incentive Publications, Inc.
Nashville, TN.

Answer Key

Page 37

our	cents	ant
meet	road	plane
inn	one	
soar	red	

Page 39

1. rugged	4. friendlier	7. brave
2. vicious	5. backward	8. angry
3. grouchy	6. proudly	9. frightening

Page 40

1. mean	4. terrifying	7. interesting, exciting
2. troublesome	5. Harmless	
3. frighten	6. friendly	8. imaginative

Page 44

1, 4, 2, 3

Page 48

1. four	5. apples
2. three	6. butterfly
3. four	7. spoon
4. two	8. Answers will vary

Page 50

Facts: 2, 3, 4, 8, 10, 13
Opinions: 1, 5, 6, 7, 9, 11, 12, 14

Page 54

1. Moondrips Shampoo
2. magnet
3. "Solar-shock"
4. Star-Struck Store
5. $3.95 per bottle

Page 62

Blueberry, bran, corn
Cream-filled, jelly, maple
Apple, pecan, pumpkin
Carrot, coconut, devil's food
Chocolate chip, peanut butter, sugar
Raisin, rye, wheat

Page 63

Page 64

Across
  2. question
  3. comma
  5. exclamation
  6. sentence
Down
  1. period
  2. quotation
  4. period

Page 69

Draw a mountain behind the barn and add a door and two windows to the barn.
Draw two cows, a horse and six chickens around the barn.
Add three more animals to the barnyard scene.

Language Literacy Lessons / Reading Elementary
Copyright ©2002 by Incentive Publications, Inc.
Nashville, TN.